DORIS LANGLEY MOORE published her first book in 1926, and is still at work. She has written six novels, several works on aspects of style and the history of costume (the study of which she has also promoted by organising exhibitions and giving lectures), and two important books about Lord Byron. She has done varied literary work in connection with films, television and ballet, and has designed clothes for period films. In 1955 she founded the great Costume Museum in the Assembly Rooms at Bath, to which she remained for many years Adviser.

Doris Langley Moore's
BOOK OF SCRAPS

New Verses for Old Pictures

in association with
ANDRE DEUTSCH

First published 1984 by
André Deutsch Limited
105 Great Russell Street
London WC1
Copyright © 1984 by Doris Langley Moore
All rights reserved

Printed in Great Britain by
W. S. Cowell Ltd, Ipswich, Suffolk.
ISBN 0 233 976221

To be frank, I should never have called it respectable
To live in a basket, however delectable,
Especially if only my head were detectable.

To place children in hearts — is such conduct defensible?
I think it is horrid and incomprehensible.
If they like it themselves, then they cannot be sensible.

Sending children by post is not thought justifiable
Unless you are sure that the children are pliable
And the make of the envelope really reliable.

When I was a child
I never dared
To play with boys.
They were so wild,
They made such noise
Indoors and out —
And I've no doubt
They seldom cared
To play with me, the little churls!
So I liked girls.

Girls did not shout
And bang about —
At least not often —
And hearts would soften
To see them with their pretty toys,
Which was not quite the case with boys.

Now scrap-book boys are most polite
And never yell and never fight.
They're always kind
And most refined —
And oh, it is a treat to see
How well these boys and girls agree.

Although we should admit, perhaps,
They'll never leave the world of scraps,
But stay here, planted on this page,
As good as gold from age to age.

I can't recollect
(Nor can you, I expect)
When motor cars were few
And absolutely new;
When horsey folk jeered,
And pedestrians cheered,
And twelve miles an hour
Was the last word in power.

Then wise fools bent on cutting a figure
Started making them stronger and longer and bigger.
The engine grew faster and faster and faster,
Till it seemed to be saying: 'Behold! I am master!
What with car, coach or bus, you just can't do without me!
I'll alter your landscape and lives, never doubt me!
The lorries and trucks will grow vaster and vaster.
While speed is your passion I'll always be master!'

But still, of course,
We love the horse
For races and rides
And beauty besides . . .
Though the carriage and pair
And the gig have grown rare,
And a horse-drawn bus
Would cause quite a fuss.

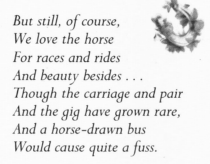

Oh for a farm that is *a* farm! —
A tranquil place of rustic charm
Where, clustering round their mother fond,
The downy chicks are kept from harm
And learn like her to scratch the soil,
And there are ducks about a pond,
And ravenous pigs whose only toil
Is eating, munching, gorging still,
And grunting till they get their fill.
(It's a waste of words, by day or night,
To wish a pig good appetite.)

Here horses, pigs and cows you see,
With ducks and hens as used to be
When farmsteads wore a homely guise
And none was like a factory . . .
But no! I won't idealise
And say that all was jolly fun.
A farmer's work was never done
And birds and beasts could suffer then
As now from selfishness of men.
But still, it was a cosier age,
As you may gather from this page.

(I know the dogs are rather big,
Likewise the solitary pig,
Which makes the horses seem too small —
The cows and sheep, too — but recall:
It's but a scrap-book, after all.)

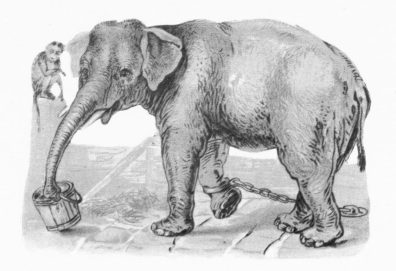

If only elephants were small
I should keep one for a pet.
I should take it on my knee
Like a little marmoset.
It would hasten at my call
To be given buns for tea.

If a tiger were the size
Of a rabbit or a cat,
I would stroke its gleaming fur.
It would sit upon the mat
Blinking with its drowsy eyes,
Breathing with a gentle purr.

I wish that lions and polar bears,
The rhino, and the zebra too,
Were built so small that they could hide
In my magic private zoo.
They would run up and down my stairs
Thinking them a mountainside.

Oh, I'd be so kind and nice
To a tiny elephant . . .
Why, then, don't I welcome mice?
You explain it, for I can't.

If you were given magical powers
To take the fruit, or else the flowers,
And make them real at your wish,
Putting the fruit on your own dish
    Straight out of the basket
    If you ask it;
Or like a conjurer on the stage
To whisk the vases off this page
So that — hey presto! — you'd be able
To have them by your place at table . . .
    Tell me your views:
    Which would you choose?

No, no, no, make up your mind!
Flowers or fruit, only one kind.
You can't have both because, you see,
There would be nothing left for me.
    Give me my share!
    It's only fair.

The hand's the emblem understood
Of service, strength, and brotherhood,
Of friendship and fidelity,
Of plighted troth and honesty.
We clasp it when we meet and part,
The lover offers hand with heart.

Three ladies and a gentleman
Are in some lamplit parlour meeting,
And each one brings a floral greeting.
Perhaps the gentleman's betrothed
To the young lady who is clothed
In white, with roses. Is it she?
Or else the one who modestly
Holds violets in her tapering fingers
Near which his own hand chastely lingers?

Or is he brother to all three?
'Tis you must solve the mystery.

Jessie and Bessie were rather dressy.
Their mothers liked them to look pretty.
Bessie's forefathers fought at Crécy,
Jessie's had prospered in the City.
But they were sweet, good-natured girls,
Fast friends, and not the least bit proud
Although their mothers both had vowed
That they should marry belted earls.

But years went by and the dear friends started
To feel for each other less tender-hearted.
Bessie noticed that darling Jessie
Was growing a shade too governessy:
She carried a Votes for Women banner,
Talked of abolishing belted earls,
And, adopting a plain, no-nonsense manner,
Lectured Bess on her frills and pearls.

Bessie was anything but compliant.
She went on the stage in a mood defiant,
Determined that she would make a name
For wearing styles deliciously dressy.
Yet friends again these girls became;
For Jessie learnt that in Parliament
Time may be as wastefully spent
As in frothy, lacy, feminine fashion;
While Bess, as an actress, soon grew tired
Of doing her hair in frivolous curls
And changing her clothes, which had been her passion.
In private life she wore serge, like Jessie.
Meanwhile their mothers, now widows admired,
Both got married to belted earls,
And so maternal ambition expired.

Which is Jessie and which is Bess
From their two portraits you may guess.
And if their mothers you would know,
Chose one of the ladies in the top row.
The other mother you'll find below.

Solemn cats and eager cats
And cats that sleep all day on mats
And lonely cats that no one pats
And cats that lie in wait for rats
And cats that growl and cats that prowl
And even cats that darkly howl —
All cats, yea, every single one,
Aloof or wild or full of fun,
Share some strange ancestral grace.
In nature's book the rule is written
That every cat and every kitten
Shall carry the mysterious trace
Of many an ancient feline race.

So, thoughtful child, remember this:
Each cat a little tiger is,
An ocelot or jaguar
Dreaming of rain forests afar,
A little lynx, a little sphinx
With riddles in its glinting eyes,
And answers too, if we are wise.
Oh, children must be blind as bats
Who do not show respect to cats.

I don't object to running dogs —
Or running frogs or running hogs.
If animals delight to run
I shouldn't wish to spoil their fun,
Unlike the critical Chinese,
Whom running dogs displease.

Here is a terrier black and tan,
Who runs like mad whene'er he can;
The greyhound runs much faster still,
The collie rounds up sheep with skill.
Retrievers, too, are glad to run
When work is to be done.

The bulldog on the other hand
On broad and sturdy lines is planned
To hold his ground and face his foe;
The spaniel's pace is rather slow.
For sport he does not care a rap
When snoozing on your lap.

The sport preferred by Pekingese —
The dog that really is Chinese —
Is hurtling wildly round the hall
And bouncing like a rubber ball
Into your favourite armchair
With shrieks and yelps that rend the air.
Yet though with life he's all agog,
The Peke is not a running dog.

Now what in the world can an angel do,
Floating about in a dumpling stew
Without any legs and things?
The sort of angel I like to meet
Is a smiling infant all complete,
Who knows how to use its wings.

How do these seraphs pass the day?
What kind of games do you think they play
Above the changing skies?
Some make patterns with wreaths of flowers,
Some play the lyre for hours and hours,
And skilfully harmonise.

I'm told they are very clean indeed
And absolutely free from greed . . .
And yet I think, my child,
I'd rather you would choose to be
An earthly imp that shrieks with glee
And sometimes drives us wild.

Some people think they'll never see
A poem lovely as a tree,
With which I simply can't agree.

But I'll admit, no picture vies,
However hard the painter tries,
With hues of living butterflies.

The delicacy of their flight,
Their fragile wings, so feather-light —
Who could convey that radiant sight?

Or how from flower to leaf they dart,
And quivering perch, and pause, and start
In motion that must baffle art?

And so the best I can devise
In print, is just to give your eyes
Reminders of some butterflies.

Parrots, natives of the tropics,
May not speak on many topics,
But it's most unusual
For birds to speak at all.

Some chirp or warble, others twitter,
But the parrots' lot is bitter
Since their natural talk
Is only shriek and squawk.

Who can blame their inclination
To join our polished conversation,
So well deserving imitation!

PS
I must acknowledge some distortions
Of these birds' correct proportions.
A robin would feel too much awe
To loom so large near a macaw,
And swans would surely be surprised
To meet a thrush so oversized.
And notice, too, another thing —
Winter and summer mixed with spring!

I think (but please to keep it dark)
The printer's done it for a lark.

A boat and a boat and a very pretty boat!
But what's to be done with this pretty boat?
For who would venture out to sea
In the most fantastic craft afloat?

Now this is the sort of boat for me,
And there's a pair of sailors for a boat like her —
Rather too large, I quite agree,
But that's a good fault in a mariner.

Only, now I come to think of it . . .
In a vessel that's never still
I might feel just a little bit,
A little tiny bit ill.

You *wouldn't*, I'm sure, so I'll tell your what:
You take the sensible, manly yacht,
And I'll have this perfectly silly lot.

Here are shells
With magic spells
From the seven seas.
In each one a creature dwells
Carrying with ease
The snug and private home
It built beneath the foam.

How beautiful and various
The scallop and the nautilus,
Ianthina and argonaut
And spiky murex, strangely wrought . . .
And still a thousand more
Are washed up on the shore.

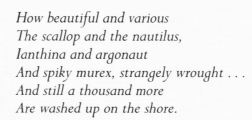

But empty, then,
Each little den,
The creature's gone.
Its house alone
Remains. It's prettier by far
Than naked shellfish are.

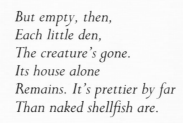

Suppose you hold against your ear
A hollow shell with smooth lips curled,
And listen quietly: you'll hear
A gentle, murmuring commotion,
An echo from that boundless world,
The wondrous, treasure-laden ocean.

Very far, very far, you must travel
To reach the curious places
Where you might see these faces.
Very wise you must be to unravel
The lore of their tribes and their races.

Would you know on the map where to find them?
Just try to guess at a few!
There's an Indian (red) from Peru.
Other redskins trail feathers behind them.
There's an Indian (brown) in a turban
From the real India which is Asia,
And a Zulu who might come from Durban.
The dark man so oddly tattoo'd
Is a Maori from Australasia.
There's a chieftain, I think, from Nigeria.
The one with the cosy fur hood
Is Samoyed perhaps from Siberia.
You couldn't have missed the Chinese. . . .
The rest I leave to you to tell.

When I was young as you I dreamed of sharing
Adventures desperate and daring
Over the mountains and the seas
In lands where these exotic peoples dwell –
Through the steamy jungles creeping,
Over windswept icefields crawling
Facing perils quite appalling –
Dreams how wildly out of keeping!
Now I'm old and stiff and slow,
They have faded long ago.
Still, they've left a lingering glow
And I thank those venturers keen
Who with cameras have captured
Many a strange and striking scene,
Holding me intent, enraptured.
Who'd have thought I could have been
Snugly in my armchair curled
While I voyage round the world?

All the pictures in this book,
On whatever page you look —
The birds, the flowers arranged in jars,
The cats, the dogs, the vintage cars,
The angels, the forget-me-nots,
The hands, the garlands draped on yachts,
The butterflies, the shells, the toys
Belonging to the girls and boys —
All these and more than I can show
were sold in sheets long years ago,
And all, wherever drawn or tinted,
Were by industrious Germans printed.
Yes, on each glossy sheet you'll see
The legend 'Made in Germany'.

Right across Europe's troubled maps
The German craftsmen sent their scraps;
And I am glad I used to stop
At every likely little shop
In country towns and grey back streets
To search for those forgotten sheets
Which, even then, were old and quaint —
And yet are still as fresh as paint.